TRUMP SONNETS

Volume 1

the first 50 days

Ken Waldman

TRUMP SONNETS

Volume 1
the first 50 days

Ken Waldman

Ridgeway Press
Roseville, Michigan

Book Design: Jerry Hagins

Ridgeway Press
P.O. Box 120
Roseville, Michigan 48066

1 2 3 4 5 6 7 8 9 10

Acknowledgments:
For this project, biggest thanks to phenomenal writer, musician, visual artist, and dancer, Mong-Lan, who hosted me in Buenos Aires for more than a week, and whose love and support helped get this off to a flying start. Big thanks also to John Romano, whose friendship and support have been instrumental when I'm not on the road (and in Breaux Bridge, Louisiana, where I finished this project). Thanks also to my earliest readers for this: Jerry Hagins, M.L. Lieber, Sunil Freeman, and Aaron Jonah Lewis. I'd also like to give a shout out to the late Phil Dacey, good friend and superlative poet who much enjoyed the George W. Bush book, and who I wish was still around so I could send him a copy and hear what he had to say. A mention, too, to Alaska friends, Jim & Martha Stey, Pat Fitzgerald & Robin Dale Ford, David McCormick, Tom Paul & Jan Caulfield. I may not be in state much, but I'm still a resident, and they always make me feel at home. There are hundreds of others I'd like to thank, including Jim Phillips and Christy Leichty of the Whirlybird. I'll try remedying the omissions the next time around.

Contents

III

An After Sonnet

To Donald Trump, from Manhattan

Vindictive, vengeful, rude, mean, petulant,
bullying, conniving, so much lying,
cheating, swindling, exaggerating,
a filthy boor, predator, miscreant,
creepy little boy, strange adolescent,
proud lecher, loud, crude, lewd, horrifying,
terrifying, so antagonizing,
thin-skinned narcissist, vicious pissant,
sociopathic, misogynistic,
appallingly unapologetic,
unstable, insatiable, flammable,
venomous old punk spoiling for trouble,
an international embarrassment,
meet Donald, the next U.S. president.

I

Trump Miami: Success

Look, people. Don't do as I do. Just do
as I say. Believe me, we're going to get
to work. I'm going to take charge and let
my team do their jobs — it will all be new
in this land we love. Like you, I love true
old-fashioned values. I'll never forget
all the super Americans I met
as I campaigned. Yes, I love all of you.
Let's be honest here. The job is real tough.
You all chose me for very good reason.
I'll tell it straight. People, you've had enough
of corrupt losers who've run Washington.
I promise a new day. I mean business.
Immigrants. Supreme Court. I'll fix the mess.

To Donald Trump, from Baltimore

You make George W. seem a statesman —
your opening trick. What the hell is next?
Enact bills to place your orange oversexed
visage on stamps and coins? Re-imagine
your university? Republican
top dog, you now own it all. Your context
in history: we've seen just how you've wrecked
all you touch. Give it time. The American
people is by far your biggest brand yet.
Count me in to see just where it all goes.
Sue the senate, your cabinet, run up debt
to Russia and China. And Mexico —
that wall. Soon appears some sweet young hussy
you'll have to grab. That's you, Donald. Fussy.

Trump Atlantic City: Salary

I'll tell you about a difficulty.
The presidency means quite a hardship
for me and my family. My earnings will dip
much because there's almost no salary,
that's why. But I've fully promised to be
the best president in history. I'll whip
this great nation back into fighting shape.
That, I'll 100% guarantee.
For the best bet of your life, bet on me.
I'll make the day-to-day of this country
hum like a hotel, a golf club, a tower,
a casino. That's my idea of power.
True, the money is lousy, a real shame.
But trust me. There are ways to play this game.

To Donald Trump, from Detroit

Donald, Donald, what is it you want?
Granted, you've a rare gift for inciting
violence, provoking infighting
among associates. How you confront
the world, brazen one. This political stunt,
your grandest hour. How you try inviting
comparisons to Lincoln. We're deciding
you're more Putin or Stalin. We can't
grasp motive. Is it merely to enrich
accounts, strengthen your brand? To pay debts?
Is there anything there after your loud self?
Donald, oh, Donald, you'll find it's a bitch,
this life in lights. Your presidential portrait:
a dark circle of oafs, you the burly elf.

Trump Long Island: Reflection

I'm not proud of having been twice divorced.
I'm not, and never have been, a racist.
My best friends know all this. But lies persist.
Many of the failing papers are forced
to make up stuff. They're so corrupt, of course.
Believe me. All they know to do is twist
facts to suit them. Look at how much they've missed
the past months. It's terrible. The poorest
record. The worst reporters. I'll just keep
being who I am. Believe me, I sleep
fine every night. I love my wife, have much
work to do. It's such a privilege, such
a joy to serve. I will unite this land,
make us proud Americans. Life is grand.

To Donald Trump, from Hollywood

In a just world, you'd be pariah —
coarse loudmouth, female-groping braggart,
businessman with frayed wallet for a heart.
But 21st century America,
there you are, commander-in-chief, and, voilà,
most powerful ruler on earth. Part
reality TV star, part surreal art
house cinema leading man — Praise Allah! —
the world seeks out treatment for injustice.
So there you are, holding court, the favors
blowing endless as wind across the globe.
In lieu of censure, you're hugged, fawned over, kissed,
you who've committed every last flavor
of sin. Just world, lift the man's veil and robe.

Trump Tower: <u>The New York Times</u>

They've been going downhill for years now.
Once, terrific. It's unfair they can write
what they do without punishment. It's not right.
I'll file suit. As president, I'm allowed
to do as I please. At last I can show
what I'm made of. People, we're made of might.
We've got first-rate armed forces that will fight
to protect us. I can fight too. The low
media blows have will to stop. My home
town paper will have to shape up. Failing
is not an option. They'll have to come
to me for stories. False talk about jailing
protesters and dissidents. Who wants to
read that crap? They'll come around to my view.

To Donald Trump, from Boston

Every day, Donald, another outrage.
That's the problem—people treat you as if
rational. You're made of different stuff.
You're from—how to say it—a darker age
where a person's sole worth is judged by wage,
where men get more respect by acting tough,
where women can never do quite enough
to be paid the same as men. Now on stage
as never before, your insanity,
Donald, is a grave national concern.
You might think yourself a Jack Kennedy,
but it's madness how you can't seem to learn
what the job entails. It's public service,
Donald. It's helping others. Playing nice.

Trump Cleveland: Tweets

For me, it's a near-perfect invention.
I can say what I want and it gets heard
by millions. A few dozen choice words.
Not much. I can do it quick. Just mention
ISIS or Alec Baldwin. The attention
is immediate. The new way forward.
Just type a fast response to what's occurred.
Like magic I have the entire nation
know my best thoughts. Why do a single press
conference when I can reach people like this?
I can say absolutely everything
I need. No hack reporters questioning
me on policy. That's Mike Pence's job.
He'll talk at length to the media mob.

To Donald Trump, from Des Moines

One well-traveled journalist described you
as sounding exactly like an African
dictator. Donald, that comparison
is no compliment. But what else is new?
You complain, cajole, humiliate, woo,
and now you sit in an office that can spin
you with extra weight. Again and again
you proclaim what can't possibly be true,
and expect us to believe you. Donald,
the dizzy pace only makes your illness
worse. You're a sick man. A half-assed ribald
businessman is one thing. Making a mess
of the U.S. presidency, another.
Oh, you'll go down, Donald. How you'll suffer.

Trump Madison: Recounts

There's something very wrong with a system
that allows for a conceded election
to be challenged. It's over. I'm the one
declared winner. What the hell is wrong with them?
Give me a break, sorry losers. Problem
after problem to deal with — transition
of power is not easy! — so it's no fun
having to listen to every news program
declare Pennsylvania and Wisconsin
recounts. And another for Michigan.
First, I'll sue the Greens. Can't delay what's been
decided. We shouldn't count votes again.
.Such corruption. When I take charge, all recounts
will be banned. That's the first thing I'll announce.

To Donald Trump: from Kansas City

Your master plan, Donald, is to somehow
thwart those dopey critics. The internet
must be restricted. That's your ace ticket
to keeping power. But how, Donald? How
to take away that 24-hour flow
of information? Raise rates, Donald? Let
providers control content? You'll regret
not taking care of this. The time is now,
Donald, before people tire of the lies.
You'll always be blaming *The Times* or *Post*,
Donald, for treating you so unfairly.
They lie, you moan. But why act so surprised
when simple research shows you're lying most
of the time? While you're at it, shut down TV.

Trump Atlanta: Threats

This is what it's like to have a target
on my back. Sore losers, every last one
of them. Winning is supposed to be fun,
but front page headlines won't let me forget
that people are mean and ugly. I'll set
them straight in due time. This once great nation
will be great again. My inauguration
will set the tone. I'll deal with internet
lies once I'm settled in. Punishment
will have to be extreme. They're a menace
the way they spew anti-establishment
propaganda. We're not playing tennis.
Let's give the dissidents a real lesson.
Aim at me. I'll show them the meaning of pain.

To Donald Trump, from Grand Rapids

Here's one more irony, Donald. Our schools
have made such efforts to halt bullying.
Yet there you are, proof that sneering, quarreling,
name-calling bring rewards. We'd be such fools
to ignore the lesson. Your daily schedule
is loaded with venomous rants, meetings,
lawsuits. Your education pick is for closing
schools, has never worked in the field. The rules
are upside-down. You say you love the poorly
educated. I'll take that literally —
that's you in the mirror. As for critical
thinking, let's not now get political.
No doubt you'll find funds to resegregate,
promote Jesus, stop ostracizing hate.

Trump Orlando: Foreign Affairs

How come I'm not seen as hale and hearty?
Aren't I universally admired? How come
such venom about where I've come from?
And Melania too. It's a sorry
world that can't just see this as a party
for America. The media is dumb —
they don't want the real story. We'll bang the drum
for America. No reason to worry.
I'll bring our friendship to Taiwan, China,
Mexico, Panama, Argentina,
Scotland, England, all of Ireland too.
Syria, Iraq, Iran, plus a few
more Mideast nations. Of course there's Israel.
I'll shake hands, tell fellow leaders how I feel.

To Donald Trump, from El Paso

Donald, you think you can run the country
exactly like your biggest new hotel,
that it's simple as buy people off, sell
naming rights, break promises, go blithely
on to the next, keep the deals in family.
Donald, once people see beneath your shell,
they'll find a sad and creepy old motel
with leaky roof, broken plumbing, creaky
floors. A building that ought to be torn down.
If they see the man managing those halls,
they'll find a sly, devious, deceitful clown
spray-painting graffiti on the outside walls,
who'll later claim it's the foul work of some
nasty hoodlum from a foreign kingdom.

Trump Dallas: Firearms

Of course I know the Second Amendment.
That's a key part of our constitution.
My job is to be myself. Protection
from intruders — we all want that. I went
all over and talked to people. I've sent
words to congressional leaders. The gun
is not going away. No American
should have to be without. My great intent
is to put in practice those principles
that make our country great. We all should work —
oil, coal, gas. We all should feel most secure.
The constitution has a lot of rules.
The courts, as I see it, are our legal clerks.
We'll keep good laws. Toss the bad. That's for sure.

To Donald Trump, from Cincinnati

Donald, Donald, a real leader will take
the blame when things go wrong, then properly
apologize. A real leader freely
shares credit with all colleagues who help make
any success. Where does that leave you? Fake
news may portray you so generously
as empathetic head of state. Bur, really,
Donald, what happens if the killer quake
hits Seattle, if a twister levels
Indianapolis, if the next rogue
rebel group kills Americans in Kuwait?
Honestly, Donald, tell us how you'll sell
your winning personality at the morgue.
Wage war on geography, weather, fate?

Trump Wilmington: Tax Returns

Let me put to rest this talk of taxes
and tax returns. There are loopholes throughout
the system and I'm smart. I'm not about
to pay more than I owe. Those are the facts.
You can go through my records: the faxes,
old emails, what-have-yous. I have no doubt
there's nothing there. My accountant is out
this week, but when he's back I'll have him track
the numbers. That will be the end of this.
Please, I've only been minding my business.
It will be my great pleasure to lower
taxes for most all. Richer and poorer
should both see immediate benefits.
We'll close down the loopholes — within limits.

To Donald Trump, from Denver

How will you finance new projects, Donald?
Raid social security? The treasury?
Revise Medicare? Privatize thirty
or forty government agencies? Hold
a Library of Congress auction? Scold
foreign leaders, demand they pay up? See
Putin for a loan? Run military
bake sales? Melt whatever silver and gold
you have on hand, then sell it all off?
Building new monuments takes lots of cash.
Repairing bridges, tunnels, roads — expensive.
Lowering taxes? Come on. What more proof
does anyone need? This is simple math,
Donald. You'll bury the country alive.

Trump Phoenix: Food

I've never been called one of those food snobs.
Fast food is fine. Or a well-done strip steak
with baked potato, and salad. I don't make
a thing in the kitchen myself. Meals rob
me of time. I'll go without, or else grab
a burger or turkey sandwich to take
on the plane. I'll have a piece of pound cake
when offered. Same with corn on the cob.
Regular food. That's what I like. I drink
coffee, soda, water, juice. Helps me think.
Of course I know my way to restaurants
as fine as any. I own many, want
to own more. My gift is making dreams
come true. The whole country is now my team.

To Donald Trump, from Seattle

It's one thing. Donald, to run a private
business. You've shown you can do as you want
with paperwork and employees. You can't
do the same as a public servant. It
doesn't work, Donald. Watchdogs will never quit
hounding you because it's their government
job to examine such things. If you don't
understand how massive this place is yet,
you will. Eyes and ears are everywhere,
Donald, and the majority of people
don't merely deeply dislike you, they hate.
You're not going to change. White is white. Square
is square (though how you try calling it *circle*).
We'll judge just how you'll make this country great.

Trump Soho: _Saturday Night Live_

They're no longer even halfway funny.
The program should have been canceled years ago.
What's with the moronic cast of the show?
They're supposed to do real comedy.
Shut them down! Put them out of their misery!
Ratings I've seen have them down near zero.
No one watches. They pay the studio
audience to attend, I hear. Money —
advertisers won't go for stupid trash.
They can't just attack me like that and feel
they can get away with it. That's not right.
Saturday night is no time to rehash
the week. It's time to have fun, relax, steal
a few laughs. The show is not very bright.

To Donald Trump, from Nashville

Donald, consider your new cabinet.
Two funny words come to mind: *motley crew*.
As if you've picked a tired metal band too.
Our joy shouldn't come from watching them get
in over their heads, the daily internet
squabbles, the inattention to taboos,
the finger-pointings, the firings. Still no clue,
you'll replace them with more cronies in debt
in some fashion. No one with intact scruples
would take such a job in your haphazard
administration. Only sorry pupils
and pals. The world is so damn huge, Donald.
Your choices are the perfect byproduct
of a President Trump. To wit: We're fucked.

Trump Hell's Kitchen: New Construction

I love how everyday I'm front page news.
I can't wait for the Trump Presidential
Library to open. A substantial
New York City monument with statues
of me and my family. Big statues
like the one of Liberty. How I'll fill
the building with photos. Taj Mahal
on the Hudson. I'll see that boats can cruise
to a river entrance. The halls, marble.
Perhaps my family's faces sculpted
right out front. This is the kind of project
this great country needs to come full circle.
We'll scout properties. I'll be consulted.
Yes! I'm already thinking architect.

To Donald Trump, from Memphis

I keep wondering, Donald, if you'll make
the finish line. Every day, new drama
of your own design. Your Alabama
man, Sessions, is typical: racist snake
as attorney general. How you'll shake
things up, Donald. You're our senile grandpa,
weirdo successor to smart Obama.
You'll talk to anyone, offer a stake
in the plans—a day or two later act
like that conversation never happened
on your way to making even more mess.
Donald, we grasp the now obvious fact
that you're insane crackpot; we can't pretend
you away. Darkness, you're darkness.

Trump Newark: Language

What is it with this word, emoluments?
No one has ever heard of such a thing,
but there's the failing New York Times finding
precious space to knock me again. Nonsense!
Nonsense! Look it up. U.S. Presidents
do what they want when it comes to having
side interests. That's the law. My team's having
a field day seeking the truth. We're against
the terrible liberal New York Times
and Washington Post, both losers, fighting
to stay in business. Nothing here to see,
but everyday they need stories. Big crimes
sell papers. Emoluments? They're writing
the dumbest story in all history.

To Donald Trump, from Chicago

Saturday Night Live will only be first,
Donald, to make us snort at your expense.
Come on. Don't you have one lick of horse sense?
(Why ask—with your strange hair, pinched face, pursed
lips, bullying sneer, orange hue, we're cursed
with the sociopathic you). Mike Pence—
radical right-wing bureaucrat, intense
conservative—is not only no worse,
but seems likably sane in comparison.
To portray you straight, Donald, it's just not fun.
So what else to do but play with obvious
truth: a clown president oblivious
to third-grade civics or diplomacy.
Donald, it's called satire and parody.

II

Trump Albany: Names

Crooked Hillary Clinton. Lyin' Ted
Cruz. Little Marco Rubio. I don't
get credit for my wit. I don't just taunt
rivals, I humiliate. Like I've said,
I'm a winner. It's why I got elected.
I'm like the Yankees. No, people. I won't
be stopped. I've always liked to be out front
and on camera. Smart, good-looking, my head
shot is great. Dandy Donald Trump. Mister
Dependable Mike Pence. The Mayor for Life
Rudy Giuliani. Brothers and sisters,
people, we're all brothers and sisters. My wife,
Melania, she's a 10. 10, I call her.
The queen. I'm the king in shiny armor.

Trump Milwaukee: Plans

What is this with conflict of interest
and blind trusts? I have our country's success
at heart. Listen to me, people. The mess
I've vowed to clean up is just the first test.
To make it right we'll need the very best
and very bright. That's how I do business.
That's why I was elected. So, the less
interference, the better. I'm abreast
of all activities. I have a job
to do and I'll do it. Believe me when
I say that I want more people at work.
No fraudulent welfare losers to rob
honest taxpayers. I want our nation
to grow. The doubts come from media jerks.

Trump Hilton Head: Crime

No, I don't endorse what my followers
have done in isolated instances.
Come on, people. Wake up. There's no chance
these attacks are my fault. What's the matter
with this picture? Every day, every hour —
crime. It can't possibly be my fault since
I've told them to stop. Fact! Try to convince
me otherwise. My mind's open. It's a horror
show out there with some very bad people
free to roam. That's my job to examine.
Muslims, very bad. Mexicans, bad too.
The examples here are quite plentiful.
What about those disgraceful American
flag-burners? Jail-time for that ugly crew.

Trump West Palm Beach: Security

A friend asked me how I can justify
keeping my family in New York City
since it costs so much for security.
Millions each month, I'm told. That's exactly why —
I'm not worth millions, but billions. So try
considering the expense a pretty
good bargain. If it takes millions to have me
come to Washington each week, that's my
prerogative as chief executive.
That's what allows me to do my best job
for my country. I eat well. Sleep well. Live
the way I usually do. No sob
stories about this money well-spent, please.
Our USA is not in a hiring freeze!

Trump Aspen: Service

As President of the United States,
I promise to serve this once great country,
make it great again. It's been so easy
to find men of fortune to demonstrate
the direction we want to go. Create
jobs, deport immigrants, and, yes, really
crack down on abortions. The pedigree
of my picks is impressive. They're all great
examples of people who've made money
and believe in a much brighter future.
The environment won't need protection —
it's been here forever. Our warm sunny
days will not go away! We'll have fewer
constraints. I've got personal connections.

Trump Louisville: Gold

When I was a boy I heard of Midas
and felt something flutter deep within me.
King Midas. That's who I wanted to be
with all my heart. Make my parents proud as
Fort Knox. And, yes, my wealth has become vast.
Now that I've hit the grand old seventy,
I see weeks rush past. Time to act quickly
to do all I can. We must beat ISIS,
make our borders secure, lower taxes,
create more jobs, follow up on campaign
promises. It will be tough, but facts
tell me soon we'll end so much of the pain
from immigration, unemployment, terror.
My golden years will change our world forever.

Trump Queens: Father

I learned so very much from my father,
who was very smart with the real estate.
So bright with money. Rent couldn't be late
or there were consequences. I'd rather
die than anger him. He'd get in a lather
if I missed directions, or made him wait
a minute or two. My father was great,
made me what I am today. No other
person had such influence. He was rich
and he was so smart. He loved to work hard
and knew how to enjoy himself. Yankee
fan because he was a winner. He pitched
deals all over. He moved fast, always forward.
Then on to the next. He really taught me.

Trump Anaheim: Advisors

I'm bringing in men and women who share
my vision of greatness. Also my children
will be involved. They're great kids. I love them,
and they'll do a great job. No, I don't care
how it looks. I'm not some Illinois mayor
talking. I'm your president. I depend
on my great team, and there's no one I can
trust more than family. What's so unfair
is not giving them a chance. It's the same
for my cabinet picks. Please let them do
their jobs. They're all uniquely qualified.
They're smart outsiders who, like me, will aim
to put our country back on top. You knew
my dealings beforehand. Don't act surprised.

Trump Columbus: Safety

I've never had so much fun in my life.
Everything I do or say — reported
everywhere. I love it. I'm recorded
on radio, TV, internet. Life
is good. Melania is the perfect wife.
I have perfect children. We're escorted
everywhere, which is great. It's important
we're safe from gunmen or some guy with a knife —
you just never know. The secret service
has been so professional. They're the best,
and I'll expand the ranks, create more jobs.
I'll defeat all terror. I'm not nervous
about ISIS and others. Let them test
our strength. Not smart! We destroy foreign mobs.

Trump Charlotte: Fortune

I'm making money coming and going
these days, and, I tell you, that's a very
good thing. It's the season to be merry.
Person of the Year! I know I'm showing
my age, but it's <u>Man</u> of the Year. Knowing
<u>who</u> I am makes me <u>what</u> I am: very
wealthy. People suffer from much envy —
a large number don't know what they're doing —
and it's why I get treated so unfairly
by the press. I have to step carefully
or they come down on me hard. My great wealth
shields me from the haters. I have my health,
which is so important. I'm happiest
when I come out a winner. That's the best.

Trump Norfolk: Vladimir Putin

At some point I'll have to thank my good friend,
Vladimir, for showing me the way. He's smart
as a whip and governs Russia with heart.
It's a large country, like ours. We attend
the same concerns. China is not our friend
in the same way, though it's still a big part
of our affairs. About Vlad, where to start —
I've gotten to know him. We need to depend
on our allies in the big wars against
ISIS and terror. It's so horrible
what they're doing. My job is to stop it,
and I will. Russia can help. It's nonsense
to think otherwise. Russians are noble.
Smart. Don't mind the press. I'm no one's puppet.

III

To Donald Trump, from Las Vegas

A few words, Donald, about decorum.
Your kids aren't to be on your transition
team *and* run a brand whose sole ambition
is to further the Trump name. That's just dumb,
yet there you are, yammering you're victim
of some conspiracy. The situation
is ludicrous, Donald. It's why you're in
so over your big head. Look, where you're from
it's okay to be belligerent, rude,
uncouth. Blaming others for shortcomings
is part of your truth. That's your family —
I understand. But when the next Trump feud
offends China, it's not about plumbing
in a hotel, Donald. It's world history.

Trump Houston: Spies

Nonsense. Dumbest nonsense I've ever heard.
The CIA absolutely are the ones
we need to investigate. Get out guns,
let them know what we think. I've never heard
such nonsense. A Russian hack? That's the word
on the street. It's dopey information.
Not true. Big lies. I won the election
fairly. I'll be president. What's occurred
has occurred. I can't wait to start a probe,
get to the bottom of this. I'll suspend
operations, put offenders in jail.
Enemies await all over the globe.
It's not just ISIS. Not just Mexicans
or Syrians. We'll lock them up. No bail!

To Donald Trump, from Annapolis

Such notions about paying contractors,
Donald. Such a record of withholding
payment for services rendered. Stinking
cheapskate, slimy operating manager,
abominable boss man, crook. Horrors
and more horrors for innocent working
people seeking their due after finishing
a job. After expressing displeasure
about quality, you don't cut the checks,
but bankrupt a whole company, threaten
lawsuits. It used to be random people
you cheated. Donald, I can guess who's next:
the governor of a state like Maryland,
or some staffer caught calling you asshole.

Trump San Jose: Twitter

It took me awhile to learn how to tweet.
One of the very best technologies
of our time. It helps the economy
go real speedy. I like to move fast, eat
on the move, treat good friends to a nice suite
at one of my hotels. If I could guarantee
them bogey-free rounds of golf, believe me,
I would. I really can't believe how neat
that Twitter is. All my people use it
and I can't recommend it too highly.
It proves all you need is a little bit
of information. Too much makes me jumpy.
My mind is very fast. It moves around
non-stop. Twitter's quick. Keeps me on the ground.

.

To Donald Trump, from New Orleans

Watching you, Donald, is watching a train
wreck in slow motion. We'd like to avert
eyes, but can't. Gentle people will be hurt
the most. Such a monstrous crash. Once again
we look. Such a locomotive. The pain,
cruelly cataclysmic. We've all lost shirts
of course. And such blood. Blood soaking hard dirt
that first will come down as drizzle, then rain
like we haven't witnessed since the bible.
Recent floods will feel quaint and curious
as swimming holes. It's one hell of a ride
to the bloody depths. Oh, we're in trouble,
Donald, you as engineer, furious
as the train begins its long, fatal slide.

Trump Indianapolis: Television

*It's getting boring, the Sunday talk shows,
the questions. I still like doing make-up,
and being on TV. But they've got to drop
the hard-liners. The truth is no one knows
about hacking. These days the toughest pros
could be some 18-year-olds with a cup
of coffee in college dorm rooms. Our top
people know the challenge. They're on their toes,
but it's a very complex world out there.
I promise I'll do everything I can
to keep us safe from threats. It's not easy.
You have no idea. They don't fight us fair.
They're very bad people. But I'm certain
we'll win. Keep watching me. Listen to me.*

To Donald Trump, from Kalamazoo

Already, Donald, your shenanigans
are catching up with you. Strange pronouncements
on TV. Weird tweets. All the elements
of madness. Who are the unprincipled men
and women enabling you? They're your friends?
And what about family? The nonsense
you spew does not inspire confidence,
Donald. Most of us use a simple lens —
and view a man who is in no way fit
to lead the nation. Have doctors ruled out
dementia? Nothing would surprise us now
though it's a reasonably certain bet
today you'll utter something false without
a worry. Donald, take another bow.

Trump Austin: Remorse

I heard said I've never apologized.
I was sorry for private locker room
talk that was so wrongly leaked, and was soon
forgotten. I was honestly surprised
it was a big deal. Come on. No one died
and it was a long time ago. But boom,
there goes the press — with all their gloom and doom —
for one poorly-phrased remark. Let it ride,
they could have done. But no. I've said sorry,
so now we're good and I can continue
working for the United States people.
I won the vote of the majority.
of legal citizens. I know that's true.
We'll make America great! Yes we will!

To Donald Trump, from Minneapolis

Donald, the problem is pathology,
an inability to shut your mouth
and walk away, But you're so damn uncouth,
Donald. No, not smart. The psychology
says to just treat you, Donald, as stodgy
six-year-old who's just lost a front tooth—
the tooth fairy, Donald, is flying south
like Santa for you, an apology
in the form of gold coins. Donald, Donald,
what to do with you. Private citizen
Trump, the world can handle. Let him go build
and name tall buildings. No trouble. The man
as president? Smiling, he'll blow up land
and sea to resolve slights, real or imagined.

Trump Brooklyn: Taxes

Always such talk about releasing tax
returns. If what I'd done was illegal,
I'd be locked up. It's such a beautiful
system in this country. Why I catch flak —
I think it's jealousy. I'm worth the max
and people wish they were me. Most people
envy me, and they should. A beautiful
wife. Beautiful kids. These are simple facts.
If others could make my kind of money —
and if they were smart — they'd do what I do.
Some taxes will always be necessary.
It's nothing new. But it takes a top crew
of accountants to make my really big
income go away. I'm smart. I'm no pig.

To Donald Trump, from Sacramento

Donald, your pet electoral college
is mulling how to undo the result.
Will they? Once again, Donald, it's your fault
that you just can't sit still at the edge
of a cliff, but have to lean over, dredge
another round of drama. You're a dolt,
an idiot. Imbecile. Donald, guilt
means nothing to you. The truth? That's a wedge
to use like any other club in your bag.
How you keep raising the ante, daring
people to slap you, dumb clueless bastard.
It doesn't work that way. Our U.S. flag
is just some cloth. Other flags are flying
across the globe. You'll fall hard, Donald. Hard.

Trump Tampa: Election

I like to keep people guessing. I love
the electoral college. I used to
hate it. But I can change my mind. It's true
despite what critics say. So I push, shove,
live to have my way. In the end, above
all, I win. I wouldn't mind a brand new
election; I'd win again. Get a clue,
people. This is who I am. I'm a dove
when the doves win. I'll govern as I will.
I'm the president. Not the crooked Hill
who can't manage her email. Or a map
of the electoral college. The crap
about popular vote? I won that too
if you want to know the truth. Or don't you?

To Donald Trump, from Raleigh

Donald, the more I read of your strange ways,
the more mythic you become: you're truly
rebranding yourself, making history.
Simple villain, you're perfect for these days,
this absurd 21st century maze
of non-stop information. *Look at me*,
you roar. Or plead, Or, god forbid, decree.
Madman, swindler, con man. The names don't faze
you, Donald. I recall an old college
acquaintance who tossed an empty bottle
at a group, then turned away as surprised
young men found glass shatter by them. Enraged,
the group shouted back. I asked the bottle-
thrower: Why? *It wasn't me*, he replied.

Trump Reno: Happiness

Now that the electors see things my way,
I've added personal security,
and I'll keep hiring. I'm essentially
the king, even if that's not what they say.
I've never been so happy. Every day
there's so much work. I'm absolutely free
to try my best ideas. So much money
everywhere to spend. It won't go away —
I'm well aware of future benefits
and accounts that are huge. My cabinet
all have made fortunes, They'll maximize yield
for the greatest good. They're my trusty shields
I can replace at will. I have many
more good men to choose from. I know plenty.

To Donald Trump, from Omaha

The conflicts of interest are thoroughly
reprehensible. New revelations
daily, Donald. Obscene machinations
for anyone who studies history.
It's absurdity. Or a poetry
of sorts. Or comedy. Your damnation
of common morals—congratulations!
God, Donald, how did you get so filthy?
Environmental protection can't mean
the elimination thereof. Between
your picks for labor, energy, health,
justice, we see white men of extreme wealth,
objectionable pasts. This agenda,
Donald. Why do you hate America?

Trump Savannah: Russia

Russia, Russia. That's all I hear about
these days. I'm no puppet. Not a puppet
of Putin or anybody else. Mitt
Romney never heard such libel. I doubt
he ever has had a tenth of my clout
despite his wealth. Russia, Russia. Who'll spit
on Russia for me? Forget about it
already. Not a puppet! I'm about
making America great again. That's
who I am. I'll say it aloud again
and again. Let's make America great!
Enough with the slander. The Democrats
are sore losers. Hell, they don't know when
to quit. At least Harry Reid's gone. Ingrate!

To Donald Trump, from Flint

Donald, this is what's going to happen—
you won't like it, how you'll be publicly
shamed wherever you dare go, how you'll be
mocked and booed. Your life will be no tap-in
birdie, Donald. No. Forget the clapping
you think you deserve. The majority
voted against you. Your first appointees
make your foes hate even more. Some contend
you'll soften, but even your supporters
now pause. Dissent comes from all quarters,
Donald. The country is so much bigger
than you think. You can't just pull a trigger
and make them all go away. You think
you'll jail them? Bomb them? Donald Trump, you stink.

Trump Philadelphia: College Days

I loved my Wharton days in West Philly.
Penn was a great place, a train ride away
from the city. I'd get up every day,
attend classes, breeze by with A's and Bs.
It's Ivy League. A university
for smarter students. Some weekends I'd stay
at school to attend a game, maybe play
cards before some dormitory party
full of Villanova and St. Joe girls.
The Pennsylvania men were always ones
they wanted to meet. Those were some fine nights.
The best coeds like perfectly formed pearls.
Each kegger another occasion
to find someone pretty, make her face light.

To Donald Trump, from Berkeley

Donald, how I wish you'd just go away,
leave us alone. Your great accomplishment:
to spur protests from a mass discontent
never before seen in the States. The way
forward is to march, shout, write every day
and night. Donald, you're the double agent
of change, so change we must. We can't be silent
before you. You think it's a one-act play,
settling scores, owning such a grand platform
to air your mostly imaginary
grievances. No, Donald, it's your Fordham
again. This isn't your place. We worry
because you don't read, think. You're the creepy
kid who flunked literature and history.

Trump Buffalo: Co-Writer

Let me say a few words about that moron,
Tony Schwartz. I gave him his biggest break,
let him co-write my book. For his sake,
I hope he still can run. The target on
his forehead is tempting. Such a moron!
Ungrateful! And he wasn't slow to take
part credit or deposit the check. Fake,
he's a fake. Don't even bother to listen
to him go on. The most tiring old man
on planet Earth. Slander. Libel. All lies.
I should have left his sad name off the book.
He's the exact kind of American
we should deport. Traitor! He takes the prize
for hypocrisy. I made him rich. Crook!

To Donald Trump, from Hartford

By god, Donald, you're the quintessential
con artist—anybody who voted
for you, yes, you took them in. Your bloated
sense of entitlement—despicable.
Those in your camp lack basic critical
thinking skills, or are themselves devoted
fraudsters. Either way, it's duly noted
you're president for your own personal
profit. The greater good? *That's heresy.*
Community engagement? *A fool's gold.*
Long-term vision? *Don't be ridiculous.*
Honor? *See you in court.* Your grand fantasy
is a pyramid-schemer's. Poor Donald,
brag to us how you've become more famous.

Trump Toledo: More Threats

It's a very dangerous world out there.
That much can't be disputed. I've written
best-selling books. I'm well-known from Britain
to Scotland, Japan, Brazil, everywhere
there are smart, rich people. There's nowhere
I'm not known now. My friend, Vladimir Putin,
understands. No cute puppies or kittens.
It's lions, tigers, sharks, wolves, grizzly bears.
Terrorists, Muslims, angry suicide
bombers all threaten our shores. Immigrants
have to be rounded up and deported.
That's what I'll promise. Brave troops sacrificed
lives to protect freedom. My achievements
will be many. No more jobs exported!

To Donald Trump, from Opelousas

At Thanksgiving dinner, Donald, I bet
you wouldn't last a half-year in office.
You'd quit, die, get impeached. No, it's not nice,
mulling such thoughts. But a working poet,
it's part of my job. It means both regret
and no regret. It means a deep practice
with language and thought. It means being twice
sentimental, twice dispassionate.
How easy would it be for you to walk
away? Your greatest skill is your brash talk.
When it comes to action, you're the corrupt
king. It's impeachable, how you'll bankrupt
the country in months. I'd guess, though, you'll die
in a mishap. No clues how. We'd know why.

Trump Mobile: Victory Tour

Best idea ever has been to return
to the big halls and jam-packed arenas
to replay victory. America
deserves this time to see me in person, learn
about my presidency. We can earn
more trust. No press allowed. They're hyenas
making sad little jokes. America
deserves so much better. Trust me. I'll turn
our country around. We'll be great again.
Yes, I'd like to do this regularly,
give everyone an opportunity
to hear me live, to see me. We're all friends,
even the citizens who disagree
with me. I'll show them, too, who we'll all be.

To Donald Trump, from Anchorage

Ultimately, Donald, you and I are
not so unalike: American males
of privilege who enjoy pretty females
and TV sports, who travel near or far
to appear before a crowd, be a star
for an hour. We've both taken unmapped trails,
survived brutal lows. We both have our tales.
You, Donald, might perhaps light a cigar
before retiring to your super-plush
suite somewhere, your trophy wife. Whatever
you have won't be enough. Accomplishments?
Now you're the world's most powerful man. Gush
all you want. You're sad, selfish, will never
be happy. At least I have a conscience.

Trump Salt Lake City: The Future

All I ask is that I not be criticized.
I have too many more important things
to deal with. Just know that we're all trying
to do what's good for the country. The ride
has been long. And we have a longer ride
ahead. I can't be bothered responding
to every little thing. But they're giving
me no choice. Doesn't anyone realize
as president I can do anything?
It also means I no longer have to
sit still. I love what the Carolina
crowd is doing. I'll be considering
making my own wholesale changes. It's true!
Let's all make a greater America.

To Donald Trump, from Boise

I'm certain, Donald, you have no dream life—
which mirrors your vast inner emptiness,
a soul that deflects darkness with darkness.
To think you're oblivious to the strife
you cause, Donald, is boggling. Your poor wife
number three has to be just as hopeless,
as must be your kids. Perfectly dreamless
in the relentless pursuit of wealth rife
with poverty. I'll tell you what, Donald,
I'll give to you the surreally muddled
images I awoke with this morning.
Barren landscape. Grays. Browns. Black men mourning
one of their own. A gun. A lone male wolf
gamely limping, teeing off, playing golf.

Trump Jacksonville: Dealings

The weapons are our best bargaining chip.
It's stupid not to use every last thing
to show our strength. I'm not understanding
why not make them afraid. Something to whip
ISIS into shape. China, too. One trip
should be all it takes. Strategic bombing.
Get it over with. That's the way to bring
home our troops. Destroy terrorists. Our grip
has got to be firm. We can't waver here
because our great country depends on this.
When we bombed Japan, we ended things quick.
I have no fears about this. None. No fear
at all. We have to finish off ISIS.
Terrorists are losers. They make me sick.

To Donald Trump, from Albuquerque

Donald, your embrace of meaninglessness
is fearsome. You'll say or tweet anything.
Sure, replenish nukes. It's only costing
a trillion. Just as you've run businesses
into the ground, so now the whole U.S..
Donald, your lunacy is astounding.
And no one in power is threatening
to stop you. To you, they're just words. God bless,
Donald. Nukes. As in nuclear warfare.
Donald, you'll wipe out millions of people.
In return we could lose Boston, Miami,
San Diego, or Seattle. You dare
start something and the effects will ripple.
Sure, big boy, double down. Bluff those Chinese.

Trump Doral: Golf

How come there's never mention how I crack
a golf ball? I not only have courses
world-wide, I can play the game, Porsches,
I know cars. My family and I lack
for nothing. I love to remember back
when I was just learning to golf. Horses
weren't for me. I put my inner forces
into grip, stance, swing, strike. I had the knack,
and have held my own with the touring pros,
who, by the way, enjoy my company,
and invite me to join them. I've been scratch,
but lately haven't been out much. Who knows
what's in store. I love playing my many
fine courses. Soon I'll have time again. Watch.

To Donald Trump, from Ithaca

Do you think it will all be as easy
as this, Donald? Are you kidding? Just wait.
If your alt-right fans indeed practice hate,
theirs will seem like joy compared to the ugly
incidents ahead. You're the enemy,
Donald, a madman. People don't just hate
your churlish stupidity, you ingrate,
they loathe your total being, your measly
intellect. You're such an upside-down man—
everything you say, do, or touch is wrong.
You're a brazen crook, Mr. Donald Trump.
The duty of good U.S. citizens
is to resist. We're many. Days are long.
You, sir, are going to be shamed, then dumped.

IV

To Donald Trump, from Washington DC

Contemptible, ungrateful, brazen, vile,
sore winner, foul-mouthed whiner, abusive,
unsuited, brutal, clueless, corrosive,
cruel, stupid, sick, a great big pile of bull,
heartless, aimless, cockeyed, irritable,
the worst of the worst, crooked, combative,
disgraceful, shady, venal, explosive,
snide, certifiably delusional,
wickedly simple, criminal, evil,
dumb, disgusting pussy-grabbing devil,
greedy insult to the Oval Office,
smug antihero, textbook con artist,
fearsome, sloppy, dirty, deplorable.
You've met Donald, the choice of some people.

Other works by Ken Waldman

Poetry and Prose:
  Nome Poems (West End Press, 2000)

  To Live on This Earth (West End Press, 2002)

  The Secret Visitor's Guide (Wings Press, 2006)

  And Shadow Remained (Pavement Saw Press, 2006)

  Conditions and Cures (Steel Toe Books, 2006)

  As the World Burns (Ridgeway Press, 2006)

  Are You Famous? (Catalyst Book Press, 2008)

  D is for Dog Team (Nomadic Press children's poetry book, 2009)

Recordings:
  A Week in Eek (Nomadic Press, 2000)

  Burnt Down House (Nomadic Press, 2001)

  Music Party (Nomadic Press, 2003)

  Fiddling Poets on Parade (Nomadic Press, 2006)

  All Originals, All Traditionals (Nomadic Press, 2006)

  As the World Burns (Nomadic Press, 2006)

  55 Tunes, 5 Poems (Nomadic Press, 2008)

  Some Favorites (Nomadic Press, 2009)

  D is for Dog Team (Nomadic Press, 2009)